Paulo Coelho

colors and arrives on an island of harmony."

ROMERO BRITTO
COLORS AROUND THE WORLD

BEYELER – FOR THE LOVE OF ART

© 2010, Romero Britto.
ISBN 978-0-615-25906-2
Printed in China

Creation: Mattenbach AG, Aleksander Kaczinski
Translations: English/German: Catherine Meyer, lic. phil., scientist of literature
German/English: Kaye Kirst, historian of art
Printing: Global Print Services, Inc.
www.globalprintservicesinc.com

BIRKEN-
HALDE
VERLAG

ROMERO BRITTO
COLORS AROUND THE WORLD

BEYELER – FOR THE LOVE OF ART

Contents

Legends

Measurements in inch
AB: Acrylic on board
AC: Acrylic on canvas
ADR: Acrylic drawing on canvas
CDC: Complex drawing on canvas

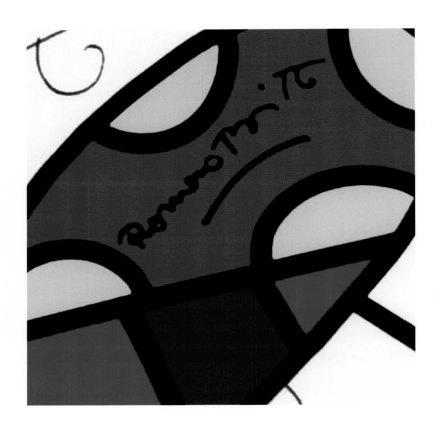

Hopeful, exuberant, enthusiastic... these are just a few of the encouraging expressions that innumerable observers, collectors, and friends assign to both Romero Britto and his dynamic works of art. Undeniably, both Britto the artist and a Britto contemporary masterpiece often are viewed through similar experiences and perspectives, since he personally evokes the same spirit of optimism and energy that is uniquely evident in his gifted creations.

Every work of art is an opportunity through which to understand the predilections of an artist, be it an ideal that the artist desires we attain or an injustice this same artist invokes society to remedy. When admiring Britto's art, we immediately sense the positive force and determination that he wielded to transform the challenges he witnessed in his youth, into the enlightened view Britto espouses today... a vision that is fundamentally optimistic about mankind and enthusiastically contagious to everyone upon whom a Britto casts its dazzling reflection.

Whether engaged in championing a global education initiative or rewarding his international collectors with a vibrant new work, I have learned infinitely from, and admired, the constants that steadfastly define Britto for more than twelve years. Indeed, the transcending artistic talent that Britto possesses is only surpassed by the generosity of his spirit. It is a joy to share professionally in the extraordinary work of Romero Britto and a privilege to call him a friend.

Alina Shriver

Romero Britto
as seen on The Apprentice,
2005

«Flying Heart» 2001

30˝x 40˝, AC

Private Collection,

USA

After visiting the Fondation Beyeler, I had the opportunity to become personally acquainted with Ernst Beyeler. I decided that when the possibility arose, I would like in some way to support him and the museum which has become a reflection of his amazing life's work and into which he has invested so much energy and passion. This decision took shape when Romero Britto generously suggested painting Mr. Beyeler's portrait and with his global art dealer, Alina Shriver, producing sixty lithographs of the portrait which would be sold in support of the Fondation Beyeler.

It is indeed an honor to be able to work towards the realization of this project, with the renowned and wonderful artist Romero Britto, as a mark of our respect and admiration for Mr. Beyeler. As is widely recognized, the Fondation requires immense financial resources in its quest to offer the public an opportunity to see amazing and one-of-a-kind exhibitions throughout the year.

We hope with this initiative it will help to ensure the future of the museum and inspire others to do likewise.

Rita Ficher Rohr

10

The success story of the Fondation Beyeler began more than 50 years ago. It also reflects the life and development of Ernst Beyeler, the son of a railway clerk, who was born in Basel in 1921. After finishing his school education and successfully completing business studies courses, Beyeler became an assistant in an antiquarian book and print dealers at number 9 Bäumleingasse, which was owned by Oskar Schloss. Always eager to learn, he simultaneously began attending lectures in both Art History and Economics.

When Mr. Schloss unexpectedly passed away in 1945, Ernst Beyeler decided that with the knowledge he had gained in this field, to continue running the business for Oskar Schloss' heirs. Only two years after taking over, Beyeler had already staged an exhibition of Japanese wood engravings, the mark of many exhibitions to come. In 1951, the antiquitarian shop was dissolved and became purely a gallery specialising in classical 20th century art with a continuous stream of exhibition activity.

Thanks to his skillful ability as an art dealer and having the courage to take risks, Ernst Beyeler purchased important works by Klee, Cézanne, Monet, Matisse and Giacometti among others, from the Thompson collection. In addition, Beyeler, who had a personal relationship with Pablo Picasso, was given the opportunity to freely select various works out of the artist's own personal stockpile, some exhibited in the museum and others added to the private collection Beyeler and his wife Hildy had begun to develop. Today, many of their private art work can be seen at the Fondation Beyeler, a gift to the community that has supported his vision for over 50 years.

The private collection of the Fondation Beyeler had its first public viewing in the Centro de Arte Reina Sofia in Madrid in 1989. This was followed by two further exhibitions in Berlin and Sydney. Since 1997 the collection has been open to the public. The collections' impressive compilation of paintings by modern masters is housed in a museum designed by celebrated architect Renzo Piano.

Patron of the arts

Ernst Beyeler

(Beyeler Fondation)

at Galerie Ficher-Rohr

2006

11

" It was fascinating to work with Romero Britto, an artist, who has a style of his own. His paintings are vibrant, colorful and full of life – and with Rita Ficher for the project of fundraising for the Fondation Beyeler also for future activities f.e. exhibitions and music. "

20 April, 2006 Ernst Beyeler

«For the Love of Art» 2006
30″x 24″, ADR
Romero Britto painted the
portrait of Ernst Beyeler, one
of Europe's most respected
art dealers and collectors to raise
funds for Mr. Beyeler's public
museum, Fondation Beyeler.
Britto is working with Galerie
Ficher Rohr, his art agent in
Basel, Switzerland, to auction
serigraphs of the portrait.

Foreword
Eileen Guggenheim
on Romero Britto

Romero Britto's paintings overflow with joy. He constructs worlds where bliss and serenity reign supreme: couples dance, pussycats smile, flying fish soar, flowers bloom and lovers kiss. To achieve such airborne emotions, Britto has invented his own pictorial language. With its brilliant colors, harmonious shapes, and pleasing patterns – his art is an art that demands to be taken on his own terms.

The joie de vivre that permeates Britto's work contrasts dramatically with the hardships of an impoverished youth. Raised in the slums of Recife, Brazil, Britto's tough upbringing might have preconditioned him to a dark or melancholic art. Despite the many adversities of his childhood, however, the artist resolved to create an upbeat art free of anxiety and fear. He has said:

"I don't believe in not talking about horrible things, but personally, I don't like to talk about the world's problems – I prefer to talk about solutions. Newspapers today provide you with horrendous stories and bad news, I believe instead, in the power of the positive message.

In my youth, life was like a nightmare. Everything seemed to be falling apart around me. Now, my art is my world. In my studio and on my canvases, I can create and control a perfect small world that I can share with everyone. Why would I want to share my nightmare?"

Britto's optimism is not only a response to his own upbringing: it is also a reaction to western art history. When asked how he was first exposed to art and what painter or image initially affected him, he replied:

"Caravaggio had a huge impact on me. My brother, who sold art books and encyclopedias, one day brought me a book on Caravaggio. Of course, I hadn't been to Europe and I hadn't seen the Old Masters before. What shocked me was the violence in Caravaggio – like the cutting of throats. I knew immediately that this represented everything I didn't want to see in my own work."

Britto has since followed a steady trajectory toward joyous subject matter. Here too, art history provides interesting precedents. In a century of turmoil, a few artists have succeeded in creating celebratory art: Britto stands squarely in the tradition of these painters. One thinks of Matisse – whose uplifting colors and designs blocked out the pain of two world wars. Likewise, Chagall's floating lovers seem to foreshadow so many of Britto's buoyant exultant couples. Léger, an artist Britto particularly admires, created optimistic, orderly scenes in a self-contained style that resists the encroachment of external upheavals.

Britto tells of admiring artists from Pablo Picasso to Jasper Johns who have consistent internal language. He talks of the tremendous sense of inner peace he achieves by being able to control all the elements of his own pictorial vocabulary. He creates his paintings by drawing an outline on the canvas, then filling in various shapes he finds pleasing with acrylics. He uses a limited range of colors and is very concerned with how they harmonize with each other. Often he will use recurring patterns, flower motifs, stripes, circles, dots, hash marks, and squiggly lines with those geometric shapes. Finally he separates the individual shapes with thin black lines. The resulting works are remarkable for their unity and consistency of design.

Britto's art is an extension of his own genuineness and gentility. Although he has divorced art from the pain and suffering that is so much a part of his century, he is not a hermit or a recluse. He believes that involvement in the community, be it local or global, is a key to personal happiness. Because Britto's art is so internationally consistent and because his themes so universally recognizable, the work transcends cultural barriers. His work as a humanitarian and a philanthropist compliments the bridge building aspect of his art.

Britto is a quiet activist. He has committed himself to numerous charitable activities. He believes passionately in environmentalism and worries about the despoliation of the rain forests of the Amazon basin. But he is always positive, always optimistic. His symbols for the Amazon: a flying fish soaring over an alligator is a supremely hopeful image and is very much in keeping with the spirit of the artist. He has said:

"I believe that every human being should try to do good for someone else. There are so many different ways to do it. My art can be an instrument for helping people... What a good feeling – that I can do that with my art..."

An art of joy and pleasure – an art that appeals to so many people worldwide – this, indeed, is Romero Britto's great gift.

Eileen Guggenheim, Ph. D.
Founder of the NY Academy of Art

«Flying Fish» 1996
80˝ x 96˝, AC
Collection of Alina and
Anthony Shriver,
USA

You were born in Recife, Brazil, what do you remember about your childhood?

Yes, I was born in Recife, Brazil. Unfortunately I don't have great memories of my childhood. I was always worried about things that a child shouldn't worry about. I use to see my mother crying all the time; my brother fighting and getting into trouble. But school was great. It was always more structured and fun than home and I loved it.

When and what was your first contact with art and when did you feel, I am an artist?

My brother used to sell encyclopedias, and I would look at the beautiful pictures in them. He would also bring home books about art and I would spend hours looking at those also. I actually started to draw and paint when I was 8 and when I was 14, I thought I could be a full-time painter, but I worried about how I would take care of my bills, and thought well I'll get a job and paint on the side. I was a practical kid. It wasn't until I was in my twenties that I knew I could probably make a living from my art.

Is there any specific artist that has influenced you?

Yes, first and foremost Picasso with his exuberant structures and figures, and also the amazing Matisse with his rainbow of colors. I became familiar with these two artists through books I read in Brazil. When I moved to the United States, I was introduced to Andy Warhol, Keith Haring, and the fantastic Roy Lichtenstein.

Rita Ficher Rohr

Why did you leave Brazil?

I left Brazil because I always dreamt about traveling the world. I wanted to learn other languages and immerse myself in other cultures. I was creative and already thought of myself as an artist, so staying in Brazil was too limited for me. I originally came to America just for a visit and ended up falling in love with my wife and the incredible energy of Miami, so I stayed for good. But I always go back to visit Brazil. I love Brazil. I also love the whole world! Traveling will always be a part of my life.

When you began to paint, did your art works have the same vibrant colors and hard-edged compositions as today?

My art reflects my need to use colors that exude happiness. I have always loved colors and from the beginning I have wanted my art and life in a certain order. That need defines the shape and form of my work.

Was the work you did for the Absolut Vodka campain integral to you becoming a famous artist?

Yes, getting the commission from Absolut Vodka really launched my career. The Absolut Vodka ad campaign put my art in front of millions of people around the world instantly. It would have taken me years of work and shows to try to reach as many people. I am thankful that since then, my work continues to reach millions more.

Roberta, Risoleta,   Brother Romolo   Romero at age 10, Brazil   Romero at age 16   Absolut Vodka Commission   Romero Britto
Romero Britto and   Britto and   and his first visit
mother Lourdes, Brazil   Romero, Brazil   to Sweden

You are from Recife, the northeast region of Brazil. Do you have something in your paintings that reminds you of the city where you were born?

In my earlier work the flavor of Recife and Brazil was more evident. Today, it's more subliminal. What someone from Tokyo can read in my paintings so can someone from the southernmost city in South America. I am trying to develop a universal language through art.

How do you think the Brazilian culture has influenced your work? Colors, style or themes?

Brazil is a country with so much ethnic diversity; there are Africans, Indians and Europeans all living together, it's a fascinating situation to grow up in. The Carnival, and the other dynamic cultural events and experiences that go on all over Brazil are an amazing source of inspiration for me.

Which person had the most important influence in your career?

The person who had the most influence on my career was Brazilian artist, Francisco Brennand. I grew up seeing his art all over Recife. I love his art.

Did you have a special dream when you were a child? Which one was it? Did it come true?

Yes, I dreamt of having a place I call home, because I grew up in a slum.

And nowadays? Do you have some other dream?

Today, my dream is to continue to paint until I die and to share my art with millions of people around the world. I would like to help and inspire people with my art.

Who is your favorite artist – painter, sculptor or designer?

My favorite painter and sculpture is Picasso. My favorite fashion designer, Issey Miyake.

Have you ever studied Art? Where and why?

I never went to art school. There was no such thing in Recife, where I grew up. I think it's great to learn about art history, techniques, etc., but we cannot forget that in the end one needs talent in order to take flight and expand creatively as an artist. The skills are important, but without creativity and talent one cannot evolve.

Are you autodidactic?

Yes, as I said before, I never attended art school, so I had to teach myself. But much of it came naturally to me.

Which of your works do you consider the best one?

The best (I think) pieces I've done so far were the six paintings I did for the United Nations Postage Administration. They were made into millions of stamps. The most challenging sculpture that I have done to date was the «Welcome» sculpture, which is 45 feet tall and was built with 15 tons of aluminum, and is now the largest aluminum sculpture in the world. The most fun I had was the conceptual sculpture I made which is now part of the famous Braman Art Collection in Miami Beach, Florida.

  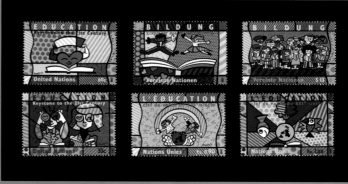

Romero Britto

showing his work in London

in the late 80s

«Welcome»

Sculpture, Miami Florida,

2004

UN Stamps,

1999

19

Some critics say that your paintings are too commercial. What do you think about that?

I guess it is okay for everything in the world to evolve and develop in all areas, but unfortunately, it seems, not in the visual arts. A few people have called my art commercial because it evokes such positive emotions and is bought around the world. I am thrilled my art makes others happy.

Do you think a strong commercial drive is against the expression of art?

It is important to have passion and discipline. When you have both, financial success will follow.

You help charitable organizations worldwide with your artwork, why?

With all the opportunities I have been given, I think it is imperative and important to help those in need with my time and art, if I can. There is so much to do – in terms of helping others – but so little time.

What were you invited to speak about at the World Economic Forum in Davos?

This year I received an invitation from Klaus Schwab to speak on four panels at the World Economic Forum in Davos, Switzerland. The panels included «Artists' Perception of a Changing World», and «The Pioneering City», and each tackled the role of art and artists in the globalization movement. It was a huge honor and an amazing opportunity to be a part of such a great event with cultural, political and corporate leaders from around the world including Bono, Paulo Coelho and J. Allard of Microsoft among others.

You met Mr. Ernst Beyeler, renowned art dealer and one of the founders of Art Basel, was it a special meeting for you?

Meeting Ernst Beyeler was an historical event for me. Mr. Beyeler is a phenomenon in the art world and it will be a long time before we will ever again have an art dealer and collector with such a passion for the arts. I think Mr. Beyeler is a God of Modern Art. Meeting him, listening to his wise words of encouragement, was very special for me.

What does it mean to you to design the invitation and to create a sculpture for the 40th Montreux Jazz Festival?

For me to be asked by Claude Nobs to create a monumental sculpture in commemoration of the 2006 Montreux Jazz Festival is a huge honor because I love jazz and the Montreux Festival is legendary. It is the second time they have asked me to create a piece of art to represent the Festival and it is a pleasure to do so each time.

Ernst Beyeler and Romero Britto
at the Galerie Ficher Rohr,
Basel

Romero Britto and
Bono at the WEF 2006,
Davos

Jazz Festival Montreux,
1999

A Brazilian Fairytale

Thanks to his Pop Art, Romero Britto escaped the Brazilian ghetto. Today his paintings are hanging in millionaire's mansions.

Daniele Muscionico

Romero Britto embodies the preconception of a European intellect as to how a Brazilian philanthropist should appear: when Romero Britto speaks, the temperature of the room rises by several degrees and a smile rises over the edge of a sunshine yellow pullover. However, Britto as a person does not necessarily comply to this first impression. He is one of the most well known Pop artists of our time – who has been invited to the WEF, is on friendly terms with Nobel Prize winners and is acquainted with Ernst Beyeler in Switzerland – when we consider the experiences he has incurred during his life it causes our western notion of wealth and happiness to falter. Feeling insecure by the heartfelt open manner of his speech, one searches for the sturdy presence of the coffee cup. Fully aware of this sudden insecurity, Britto generously praises the standard of Swiss coffee. Should it be up to one of the most successful Brazilian artists, to remind us of how to show respect towards a stranger?

Britto is staying in Switzerland, as he is taking part in the Charity Gala at the Zurich Hallenstadion on Sunday, to mark the close of the Handball Championship. One doesn't doubt for a moment the sincerity of his engagement as he is a personified example of happiness. An angel must have been watching over Romero's cradle, when he was born as the eighth of nine children in the ghetto of Recife in 1963, with no prospects of ever leaving the misery and the stench behind. Already as a child he felt drawn to color and scribbled on anything he could find, as well as showing quick-mindedness. He loved books, wanted to learn and go to school! A scholarship enabled him to attend a private school and so in his *"bleak childhood a door opened to another world"*. In 1989 a certain Michel Roux pushed this self-taught artist through the door right into the international spotlight: Roux the inventor of the Absolut Vodka Campaign, had already worked with Warhol, Haring and Ruscha, now he engaged their legitimate heir, Britto. Since then this Brazilian has been hailed as the star of "Neo Pop Cubism". When working for companies such as Movado, Evian, Pepsi-Cola and Apple, Britto was consequently condemned as being a commercial-minded artist... But how else could he reach the masses with his saturated colors to convince them of the value of the simple things in life, of happiness and of just being alive. His fellow countryman, the writer Paulo Coelho, uses nothing but enthusiastic metaphors, when speaking about Brittos lively and vivid style.

Today the Brazilian artist runs his own art-enterprise, with 60 employees on his payroll: assistants that apply the colour to the paintings; photographers, packers, drivers. He is proud nowadays, to be able to include Michael Jordan, Arnold Schwarzenegger and André Agassi, not only to his list of friends but also to his collectors. He owns studios in New York, São Paulo and Miami Beach – but still prefers to be where he belongs: with the colors. He says he owes everything to them. With them he gives himself (and us) what he must have been missing in his childhood: happiness and it is indeed through the colors that Romero Britto can relate to us this chapter in the second part of his life.

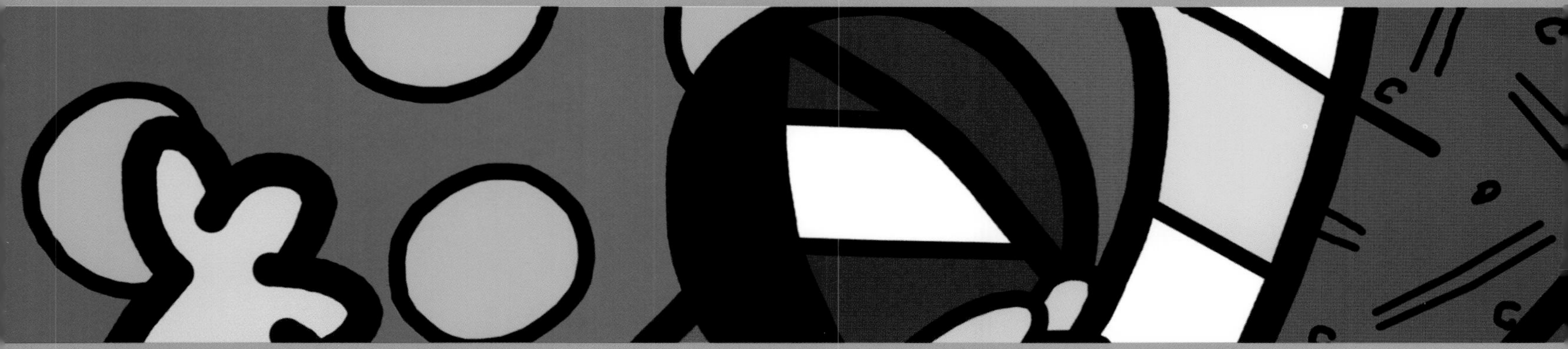

Blue Dog (Azul) for the Basel Children's Hospital

Basel's Blue Dog Sculpture

Britto unveiled «Azul», an aluminum sculpture

six and a half feet tall depicting a

happy and playful puppy created especially

for the Basel Children's Hospital

Dear Mrs. Ficher Rohr and Dear Mr. Britto,

It is my great pleasure to welcome you both. Today is such a joyous occasion thanks to your great generosity, because you have decided to donate a sculpture to the University Children's Hospital, Basel. I must say, it is not that we only rarely receive a present, but rarely does a present suit us as appropriately as this does.

Everyone in our hospital must surely be impressed by your works of art, Mr. Britto. The joy towards your work is not just superficial but lies deep within. It is as if your art causes something to move inside us, and this connection exists for both young and old. I remind you all that this impressive work of art is dedicated, above all to our children. Although a stay in hospital is no longer the frightening experience it once was, it can still be a major trauma in the life of a child and his or her parents. In this difficult situation this friendly dog can take over the role of a great friend to a sick child. But more than this, everyone will be delighted to meet him, whether it be former patients, hospital personnel or even the many pedestrians who pass by the Children's Hospital each day.

However, the significance of this donation extends well beyond this. This present is proof of the strong anchoring of the UKBB and an unmistakable symbol of its recognition and attachment in the region. As long as artists and benefactors continue to think about children, then there surely remains hope for our society. So dear Mrs. Ficher Rohr, and dear Mr. Britto, on behalf of our staff and children, it is my great pleasure to thank you most heartfully for the Blue Dog!

Dr. Konrad Widmer
Chairman of the Board

In 2006, Claude Nobs, founder and director of the Montreux Jazz Festival personally asked Romero Britto to create a monumental sculpture to commemorate the 40th anniversary of the Festival. The sculpture is permanently installed in Montreux. It was the second time, Nobs has collaborated with Britto. He also approached the artist in 1999 to create and paint an original image that would capture the essence of the Festival that year.

Founded in 1967, the Montreux Jazz Festival has established itself as one of the most prestigious annual music events in the world. The extraordinary list of artists who have played in Montreux is drawn from across the musical spectrum and from around the world.

In the last few years, Montreux has hosted over 200,000 visitors and created a forum for some of the world's biggest musical acts. Alicia Keys, KoRn, The Corrs, Sean Paul, Dido, Seal and mythical performers like BB King, Carlos Santana, Dr John, Solomon Burke, Van Morrison, Patti LaBelle, Jorge Ben Jor, Buddy Guy, Deep Purple, Cheap Trick and Chic have all played at the festival's largest hall, the Auditorium Stravinski.

The Miles Davis Hall has created an environment of diversity for a blend of numerous styles in which rock, electro pop, hip hop, reggae, world music, soul, R&B, rock, pop-folk have been honored. PJ Harvey, The Black Eyed Peas, The Roots, George Clinton, Mark Ronson, Joss Stone, Tony Allen, The Scissor Sisters, Michael Franti, Doctor L, Amp Fiddler, Suzanne Vega, Kings of Convenience and many others have played there.

«Montreux Jazz» 1999

90˝ x 60˝, AC

Collection of the artist

MONTREU

SOUNDS

«Montreux Jazz» 1999
48″ x 60″, AC
Collection of Claude Nobs,
Switzerland

Handball Charity, 2006

48˝ x 36˝, ADR

Romero Britto created
an original painting that
would honor the Euro 06
Handball Championship.

Collection of Family Thaler,
Switzerland

The Handball Charity

One of the biggest events in Europe, the Handball Championship, Euro06, hosts 47 matches in five Swiss cities. In 2006, organizers of the Championship asked Romero Britto to create an original painting that would honor this very prestigious, well-attended and long-standing sporting event. In addition, Britto was honored and his art work auctioned at a charity dinner – organized to raise funds for a handball camp held in Switzerland – attended by former Swiss president, Adolf Ogi and other politicians, athletes, entertainers and socialites.

The Handball Championships were launched following the conclusion of the highly anticipated Swiss Handball Camp in 2005. The Camp invited players from around the world including China, Israel, Iraq, Japan, North Korea, South Korea and the U.S. to spend a week together and train in the country's National Sport Center. After training, the 24 players, now forming two teams, tour and play throughout the country all leading up to a final game between both teams in conjunction with the "Swiss Handball Day Event".

The Handball Camp, endorsed by President Ogi, now a special advisor to the United Nations Secretary-General on Sport, Development and Peace, was held to contribute to the United Nations' "International Year of Sport and Physical Education", and to encourage dialogue between athletes from each participating nation.

The Handball
Championship,
February 2006

Handball Charity
Event in Zurich,
February 2006

Unveiling of
Romero's Handball
Charity Painting

Romero Britto
and the former President
of Switzerland, Adolf Ogi

J. Allard of Microsoft
with Romero Britto

U2's Bono and Britto

Britto at the World
Economic Forum in Davos

Romero Britto spoke on two panels at the World
Economic Forum in Davos, Switzerland, attended
by corporate, political and cultural leaders from
around the world. The World Economic Forum took
place from January 25–29, 2006.

Britto, along with New York's Museum of Modern
Art curator, Paola Antonelli, spoke on the panel,
«Artists' Perceptions of a Changing World». The
panel explored how art is driving globalization,
how artists react to various global influences and
asked if artists can play any role in addressing
societal issues. Romero, along with architect Rem
Koolhaas also spoke on the panel, «The Pioneering
City», which examined city centers of global creativity and how artists contribute to these cities.

At the forum Britto interacted and had discussions
with several cultural leaders including U2's Bono,
Michael Douglas, Professor Elie Wiesel, one of Xbox's
creators and Microsoft vice president, J. Allard,
and Brazilian writer Paulo Coelho among others.
*"I had a chance to speak with Bono, with Michael
Douglas and Angelina Jolie"*, explains Britto, *"and
their common desire was to make the world a more
inspiring and inclusive place in small and large ways."*

"After Davos, I've learned", Britto adds, *"that art
has the ability to uplift and inspire and the globalization of art is inevitable and welcome."*

Donald Trump's The Apprentice/ NBC Television

Two of the final four candidates from NBC's third season of "The Apprentice" had the opportunity to work with Romero Britto to create an original design to *"commemorate fifty years of t-shirts being cool"* for the Hanes company. Britto's hands-on creative task aired on NBC television on April 28, 2006.

Britto found the Apprentice task quite challenging. He had to create a work of art under a tight deadline and in a corporate office rather than his art studio. But Romero quickly became comfortable with his assigned contestants, Kendra and Craig.

He became even more enthused after visiting Scoop, a downtown New York clothing retailer, where the t-shirts would be sold the next day. *"For me it was a great experience being associated with the show. It's a show where participants can learn a lot of things: How to conduct business and how you can succeed in a world where only a few get to the top",* explained Romero.

"The Apprentice" is produced by Mark Burnett Productions in association with Trump Productions LLC.

Romero Britto shines in Shanghai

Six thousand years ago, Shanghai was the site of Songze Culture. The Jin, Yuan and Ming Dynasties soon followed and continued to fascinate the world with their culture and art. Today, this fascinating metropolis has embraced Romero Britto as one of the main artists in the Shanghai Art Fair 2005 and the Shanghai International Biennial Urban Sculpture Exhibition 2005.

From students to business and political leaders to some of China's most well-known art collectors, Romero drew the admiration and curiosity of thousands of visitors of the Shanghai Art Fair. For many who visited his space at the Exhibition, it was hard for them to resist his bright colors, vibrant geometrical forms and the vitality and energy inherent in his art and led to their first purchase of a Pop art painting.

To bring Romero's art to Shanghai was for us an act of recognition, gratitude and friendship, but what we never imagined was the satisfaction, joy and happiness that it would bring to us and so many others.

Your friends forever,

Amarilis and Claudio Osorio

«Sisters» 2005
48˝ x 60˝, ADR
Private Collection,
Shanghai, China

«For You» 2001
58˝ x 72˝ x 12.5˝,
Enamel on aluminum.
Sculpture exhibited in the
2005 Shanghai Biennale

Roger Federer Portrait

In March 2006, Romero was asked to paint a portrait of the world's number one tennis player, Roger Federer. The portrait was requested by sports host, Jim Berry of WFOR Television, a CBS-owned station in Miami, Florida. Berry wanted to honor both men as one artist to another – Romero's artistic abilities which are recognized around the world and Roger's style of play which some may view as art in its own way.

The painting was presented to Roger Federer by Berry after he won his quarterfinals match against James Blake in the NASDAQ-100 tennis tournament in Miami. WFOR produced an entire segment on Romero and also recorded a greeting from Romero to Roger. Roger was surprised and pleased. After watching the greeting and receiving the portrait, he said: *"I must meet Romero. This is so nice."*

«Roger Federer» 2006

24″ x 36″, ADR

Collection of Roger Federer,

Switzerland

Romero Britto and Best Buddies International chairman and founder, Anthony Kennedy Shriver joined forces to kick off the launch of Best Buddies, Germany. To honor the occasion, Britto captured a moment in history with his painting, «John F. Kennedy», which was presented to the new Chancellor of Germany, Angela Merkel, at an exclusive ceremony on November 30, 2005 in Berlin.

The original artwork was presented to Chancellor Merkel and the people of Berlin as a tribute commemorating President Kennedy's *"Ich bin ein Berliner"* speech which took place at the Brandenburg Bridge in 1963. In addition to the unveiling of the highly anticipated JFK piece, Britto also dedicated an original image of "Children of the World" to Best Buddies. This inspiring image was reproduced into a new release serigraph.

«President John F. Kennedy» 2005
24˝ x 16˝, ADR
Romero Britto paints an original for
the launch of Best Buddies Germany.
The piece was presented to the
Chancellor of Germany.

Romero Britto
with German Chancellor,
Angela Merkel

Biennale Interna-zionale Dell' Arte Contemporanea, Firenze

The Internal Selection Committee of the Florence Biennale extended an invitation requesting Romero Britto's participation in the fifth annual International Biennale of Contemporary Art, which was held in early December, 2005 in the exhibition hall of the historic Fortezza da Basso in Florence, Italy. More than 2,000 artists have participated in the Florence Biennale since its inauguration in 1997. In 2001, the United Nations recognized the Florence Biennale as an official partner in the program, "Dialogue Among Nations", which utilizes cultural riches present in an assortment of societies worldwide. The program supports dialogue through universal acceptance and observance of cultural diversities in an effort to foster the advancement of peace in environments of cultural unrest. The steadily increasing number of participating artists demonstrates how this particular program has found a voice within the structure of the Florence Biennale.

In 2003, 890 artists from 72 nations, despite their differences of language and faith, found a common language in art to communicate their cultural values, illustrating Kofi Annan's statement: *"Artists have a special role to play in the global struggle for peace. At their best, artists speak not only to people; they speak for them. Art is a weapon against ignorance and hatred and an agent of public awareness... Art opens doors for learning, understanding, and peace among people and nations."*

The body of work chosen for participation in the Biennale illustrates the unifying message of this exhibition. Romero Britto's painting, «Looking into the Future» is an immense depiction of peace amongst the masses as we advance into the twenty-first century. This piece was generously exhibited on loan from private collectors of Romero Britto's work.

46

«Looking into the Future» 2005
80˝ x 96˝, AC. Exclusively exhibited in the Florence Biennale, on loan from
the private collection of Mr. and Mrs. Gustavo G. Miculitzki

Cow Parade – New York

Romero Britto
paints cows for Cow Parade in
2000

The world's largest public art event, Cow Parade first came to New York City in 2000. The event's organizers asked Romero Britto and other world-renown artists to paint or put their unique stamp on a life-size fiberglass cow. Cow Parade, which was realized in order to bring art to the public, has also raised millions of dollars for charitable causes around the world. Since its inception in 1999, Cow Parade has been exhibited in Chicago, New York City, Kansas City, Houston, London, Mexico City, Florence, Italy and Buenos Aires, Argentina, among other major cities.

Cow Parade is not meant to be high art, however. It is first and foremost a public art exhibit that is accessible to everyone. *"Art is about breaking down barriers. It gets people to feel, to think, to react. So when you come across life-sized cow sculptures that have been covered in mirrors or gumdrops, cows that have been painted with elaborate themes or transformed into something else entirely, you can't help but stop and think about what it means. All your preconceived ideas go out the window. Suddenly people see that art can be fun and that art can be interesting to everyone, not just people who frequent museums"*, says Peter Hanig, a Cow Parade event organizer. Art for all is the same philosophy that has shaped the career of Romero Britto, making him one of the most beloved and respected artists of his generation. Britto, who donates hundreds of art pieces to over 200 charitable causes each year, was also motivated by Cow Parade's philanthropic focus.

At the conclusion of each Cow Parade event, the cows are herded up and many are auctioned, with a substantial portion of the proceeds benefiting charity. The Cow Parade New York 2000 Charity Auction raised an impressive $1,351,000 benefiting several New York City charities.

«Cat and Dog Cow»

«Butterfly Cow»

50

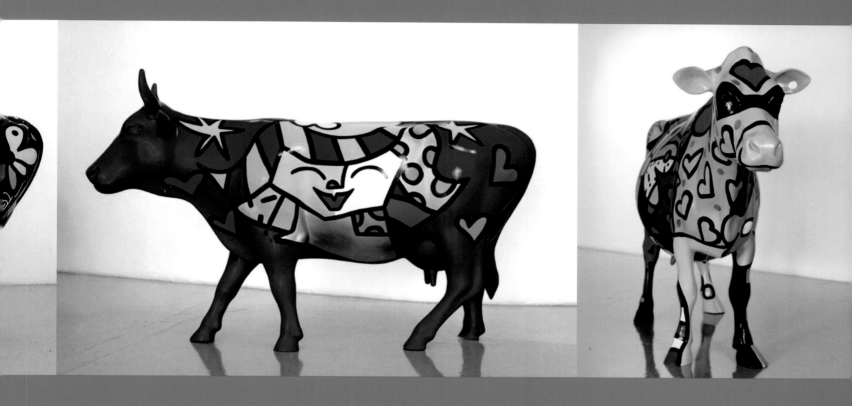

«Cow Girl»   «Moo Cow»

Extreme Makeover: Home Edition

One of the U.S.'s highest rated and most popular TV shows, "Extreme Makeover: Home Edition" (EMHE) changes the lives of a very deserving family each week by completely renovating their home from top to bottom. Romero Britto was asked by EMHE producers to paint a very special room for the Herbert family – a man who had lost his sister and subsequently took in her two children – in the resort town of Sandpoint, Idaho.

The theme of the room was "The World" because the family mentioned to the producers that they would love to visit several countries, one day, including Mexico, Thailand, Vietnam, Laos and Australia. Romero highlighted each country by enlarging them and including different details and designs that are symbolic to the country. The United States was also a large focus and included all the states, with an emphasis on states meaningful to the family such as Montana, Idaho, Hawaii and California. The globe mural covered the entire room, called a Bonus room, from floor to ceiling. The overall room dimensions were 19 ft deep by 16 ft wide and 8 ft high.

The family had no idea world renown artist Romero Britto was painting this room in their home as the home renovation is kept a total surprise until the last nail is hammered in and the final paint stroke is complete. The results were revealed on national television on January 22, 2006 with millions of viewers seeing the results of Britto's work.

Romero with Ty Pennington,
host of Extreme Makeover:
Home Edition on ABC TV

Millions of viewers watched
Romero Britto on "Extreme Makeover:
Home Edition" paint a room
for the Herbert Family in Sandpoint,
Idaho, USA. 2006

Royal Carribean – Mariner of the Seas

In 2003, Royal Caribbean International asked Romero Britto to complete one of his most ambitious and colorful works to date; the 25,000-square-foot pool deck of Royal Caribbean International's Mariner of the Seas. Royal Caribbean commissioned Britto to transform the main pool area into a one-of-a-kind art experience for its guests.

"It's an incredible coup to have an artist of Romero Britto's caliber create what is essentially an outdoor art museum for our newest ship", said Jack Williams, president and COO for Royal Caribbean International.

Britto's whimsical figures and playful patterns adorn two levels around the main pool, including the deck and wading area, pool columns, wall panels, Jacuzzi and bandstand canopies, the Pool Bar and the Sky Bar. The vibrant focal point is a 10-foot aluminum sculpture of a surfer titled «All about Fun».

Britto spent more than a year on the project, from initial concept through final construction. He traveled to Turku, Finland, where the ship was built, to hand-paint the pool deck pillars and oversee the installation of the components. His designs adorn a wide variety of materials, including metal sheets, rubber flooring, painted columns, canvas awnings and translucent plastic. For those who want to own a little bit of Britto, Mariner's gift shops feature items such as beach towels and sun visors sporting the artist's distinctive designs.

The 3,114-passenger, $700 million Mariner of the Seas is the fifth ship in Royal Caribbean's Voyager class and is the largest ship to sail from Port Canaveral, Florida, year-round. Royal Caribbean International is a global cruise line with over 18 ships in service.

«Mariner of the Seas»
In 2003 Royal Caribbean International asked Romero Britto to complete the 25'000-square-foot pool deck of Royal Caribbean International's Mariner of the Seas, the newest edition to their fleet.

The Welcome Sculpture

Standing a towering four stories high (45 feet), Miami's whimsical «Welcome» sculpture was conceived by Romero Britto at the request of developer Jeff Berkowitz for his Dadeland Station Shopping Center project.

The world's largest aluminum sculpture, «Welcome» is comprised of 15,000 tons of aluminum with over 7,800 inches of weld and also has a wingspan from open arm to open arm of 45 feet.

A fleet of extra wide tractor trailers was hired to move «Welcome» to its home at the Dadeland North Metrorail Station on Tuesday, June 1, 2004. There, «Welcome» was assembled with the assistance of a large crane, bolting and welding the numerous sections together. Following its erection, Britto mounted a bucket truck and began hand painting «Welcome.» Painting the enormous sculpture took over two weeks.

Britto was pleased after its completion which took a total of 18 months: *"This sculpture is a great way for me to share my art with county commuters and the many people who come to Dade County from around the world to shop at Dadeland Station. Hopefully, they will enjoy my work and it will make them feel welcome."*

«Welcome» Sculpture.
«Welcome» was conceived at the
request of developer Jeff Berkowitz for
his Dadeland Station Shopping Center.
The sculpture is comprised
of 15,000 tons of aluminum. It is one
of the world's largest sculptures.

«The Ice Skater»

14 x 25 feet, Aluminum

Private Collection,

Florida, USA

São Paulo International
Airport Mural.
Two murals 20 feet high by
20 feet long were commissioned
by Duty Free of Brazil and
Infraero. Over 100 million
people from around
the world pass by the murals
in São Paulo.

Baggage
Claim

Terminal 8

Ground
Transportation

John F. Kennedy

(JFK) Airport,

«The Apple»

Aluminum sculpture

60

When he took the stage at the first annual Latin Grammy Awards in Los Angeles, California, entertainer Carlos Santana paid homage to Romero Britto by playing against a backdrop of the artist's work displayed from end to end of the huge stage of LA's Staples' Center. It was the culmination of a four-day celebration of Britto's work leading up to the prestigious awards gala.

Britto, who had been commissioned to provide several elements to one of the year's most exciting entertainment events, was honored on day one with an exhibition of his work at the Art One Gallery in association with the Latin Academy of Recording Arts and Sciences. There, Romero along with record producer, Emilio Estefan unveiled his commissioned piece, «Latin Grammys» commemorating the event.

Britto's work continued to dazzle everyone attending the «Latin Grammys». Not only did his artwork adorn the stage but the second image he created for the award ceremony was featured on the night's program cover as well as the pass that allowed attendees to enter the post-Grammys celebration. A celebration attended by award performers, Ricky Martin, Christina Aguilera, Gloria Estefan, NSync and other musical acts.

Romero Britto and
Carlos Santana

Emilio Estefan and
Romero

«Latin Grammys»
Entertainer Carlos Santana
paid homage to Romero by
playing against a backdrop of
the artist's work displayed
from end to end on the huge
stage of LA's Staples' Center.

Best Buddies/
Hearst Castle

For over 15 years, Romero Britto has contributed his time and art to help raise funds for Best Buddies International, a nonprofit organization dedicated to enhancing the lives of people with intellectual disabilities by providing opportunities for one-to-one friendships and integrated employment. Britto's artwork has been auctioned to raise funds for the group and his images can be seen on Best Buddies t-shirts, cups and other collectibles. Founded in 1989 by Anthony Kennedy Shriver, Best Buddies is a vibrant, international organization that has grown from one original chapter to more than 1,200 middle school, high school, and college campuses across the country and internationally. Best Buddies programs engage participants in each of the 50 United States. The organization also has accredited international programs on six continents.

Just recently, to celebrate participants' accomplishments, Steve Hearst welcomed cyclists and celebrities to the Hearst Ranch for a barbeque and private performance by the band, The Goo Goo Dolls. More than 400 cyclists from around the country participated in the second Volvo Best Buddies Challenge: Hearst Castle, a fundraising bike ride from Château Julien in Carmel to the Hearst Ranch in San Simeon, California. The ride raised $2 million for Best Buddies' friendship and jobs programs.

Additional special guests and celebrities included Eunice Kennedy Shriver, supermodel Cindy Crawford, actor Esai Morales, actresses Kelly Hu, Linda Gray and Gabrielle Carteris, and Volvo CEO Anne Bélec. The event aired nationally on CBS Sports.

Steve Hearst's grand-
father, William Randolph
Hearst, built Hearst
castle, one of America's
largest private homes.

«Hearst Castle» 2005
36˝ x 30˝, ADR

65

In 1999, the United Nations Postal Administration commissioned Romero Britto to create its final 1999 stamp issue on the theme, "Education – Keystone to the 21st Century". The themes: economic growth, education and environment, education and health, education and family and world matters were interpreted by Britto in his own unique way. The original artwork now permanently hangs in the United Nations International School in New York City.

Britto, who was an avid stamp collector as a child, designed two stamps for each of the three countries that distributed them: the United States, Switzerland and Austria. The stamps tried to depict each culture through a variety of figures and messages illustrated with Britto's signature vivid colors, bold lines and exultant characters.

Robert Stein, head of the design unit for the U.N. Postal Administration said they chose Britto because they didn't want to approach the theme of education in a typical way, *"We wanted a nice departure from the humdrum. His work so brilliantly translated into wonderful stamps."*

And Britto was thrilled to take on the project, *"Everything is based on education. With knowledge and education you can understand the world."*

Kofi Annan

Text of statement of the Secretary General at the presentation of artwork to UNIS

Friday, 10 March 2000, 5.30 p.m.

"Ladies and Gentlemen,

I am, indeed, pleased to be here with you today and to accept on behalf of the United Nations International School one of the original paintings that was reproduced as part of the series of stamps commemorating "Education – Keystone to the 21st Century".

When I first saw these stamps last year I was struck by the vibrancy and the energy of the artwork. Education is the right of all. This artwork captured not just the myriad facets of education but also the sheer joy of learning and communicating that joy in a playful yet very meaningful manner.

I should like to express to Mr. Romero Britto, the artist, our sincere appreciation for the contribution he has made to the artistic heritage of UN stamps. This is made even more manifest, here today by his most generous gift of original artwork to the International School, which I accept with the greatest of pleasure."

SUNLIFE STADIUM

Photo by: Diego Tosoni

On August 7th 2009, Miami Dolphins owner Stephen Ross announced that Artist Romero Britto will be bringing Sunlife Stadium alive through his iconic art. Upon entering the stadium, it's hard to miss the Helixes that surround the stadium, decorated with his signature Britto work. Each gate entrance now has a signature Britto football at the top as well. "It's wonderful to have individuals like Stephen Ross who bring so much beauty to cities across the country and around the world. I'm so exited he invited me to join him on this new journey of the Miami Dolphins, where sports and art are celebrated at the same place," Romero Britto.

«Absolut Vodka»
In 2003 Romero Britto
was commissioned by
Absolut Vodka to once again
redesign its label. The new
image was distributed
around the world.

ABSOLUT BRITTO.

Absolut Britto

In 1989, Michel Roux, an executive with Absolut Vodka walked into Romero Britto's art gallery, that was then located in Coconut Grove, Florida, and was enthralled with the artist's work. Almost immediately, he asked Britto to join Absolut's impressive list of artists who had designed bottle labels for the company and contributed to a worldwide advertising campaign. It was a momentous invitation that catapulted Britto into the global spotlight and brought his art to an all-new audience.

Andy Warhol was the first artist approached to work with Absolut, his protégé Keith Haring quickly followed. Kenny Scharf and then Romero Britto were soon asked to come on board. Other internationally known artists who have worked with Absolut include Ed Ruscha, Armand Arman, LeRoy Neiman, Robert Indiana, César and Julia Wachtel. To date, Absolut's collection of contemporary art includes the work of more than 400 artists. Their work has been showcased as part of the Absolut advertising campaign and exhibited in museums around the world.

The creative nature of the Absolut brand has attracted some of the leading contemporary artists of our time to develop their own personal interpretations of Absolut. Regardless of the artist, country or type of work, every piece reflects both the vision of the artist and the spirit of Absolut.

2003

Special Edition bottle,

commissioned by

Absolut Vodka

BMW has a long history of having artists paint their cars. Roy Lichtenstein, Keith Haring and James Rosenquist are included in this prestigious group. Norman Braman, owner of eight car dealerships across the United States and one of America's leading collectors of contemporary art, has added Romero Britto to BMW's impressive roster of artists. When BMW reintroduced the Mini Cooper in 2002 it took Mr. Braman only five minutes to decide Romero Britto would be his choice to paint this "new" classic.

Norman Braman, celebrated collector, commissioned Romero for the launch of the Mini Cooper in North America.

"Romero symbolizes the vitality and diversity of Miami Beach. He has been and continues to be a very special asset to our community. Romero gives of his time, talent and resources to so many needy causes. Art is rarely agreed upon by all collectors – that's why it is so challenging. Art is rarely agreed upon by all collectors – that's why it is so challenging [but] it took only 5 minutes to choose an artist that would convey the Mini Cooper's excitement and life."

Norman Braman

Norman Braman
with Romero

BENTLEY BY BRITTO®

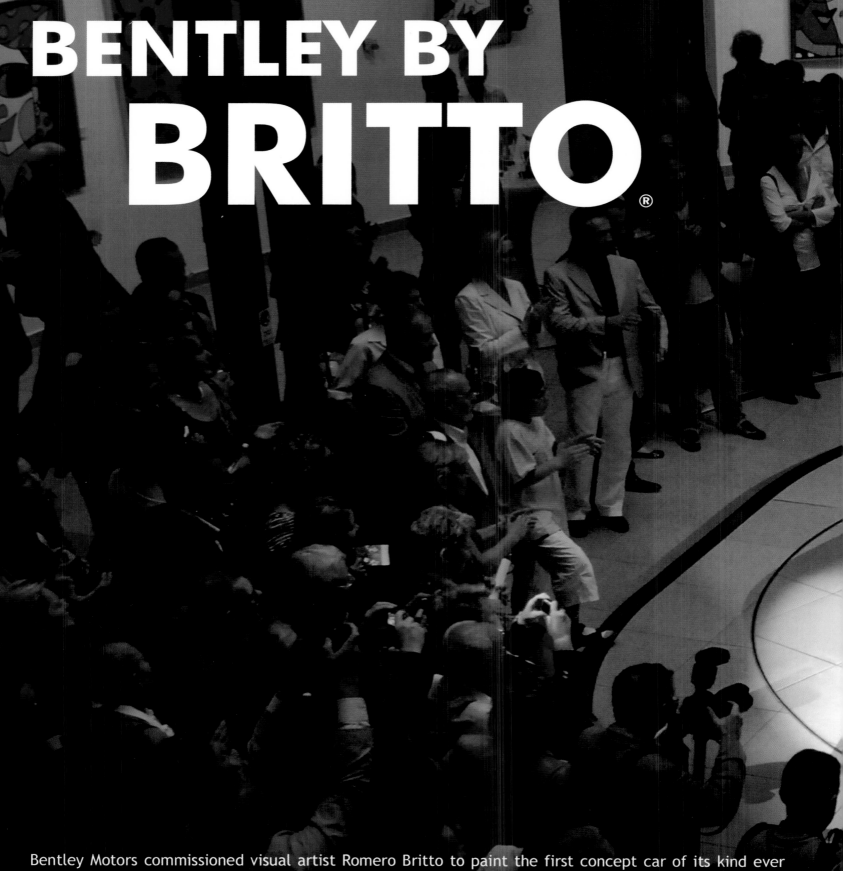

Bentley Motors commissioned visual artist Romero Britto to paint the first concept car of its kind ever designed, a prototype Bentley Continental GT. Not meant for the road, it is the one and only model of its kind. Marking the first time Bentley has collaborated with a visual artist on such a project ever in their 90 year history. This collaboration with Britto is truly a special and beautiful anniversary statement.

The Britto Bentley has appeared in more than 500 thousand news media outlets around the world. As both an incomparable luxury vehicle and as a visual masterpiece this particular Bentley Continental GT has changed the course of the 90 year old history of Bentley Motors as a company, and their future in the

Steinway & Sons invited pop artist Romero Britto to create a one-of-a-kind piano in commemoration of Steinway & Sons 150th year anniversary, for those who share the love of both Art and Music. The one-of-a-kind Art case piano is valued at $150,000. The piano was exhibited at Britto Central after returning from New York where it was unveiled at the city's annual Art Expo. Romero has been asked to display the piano at the 2006 Montreux Jazz Festival in Switzerland where he is the official artist.

For over a century, the world's most accomplished pianists have preferred to express their musical genius on Steinway & Sons pianos. The joy of owning and playing a Steinway piano, however, is not the exclusive domain of the virtuosi. Rather, it is a world open to all who share the love of music, fine craftsmanship and enduring quality.

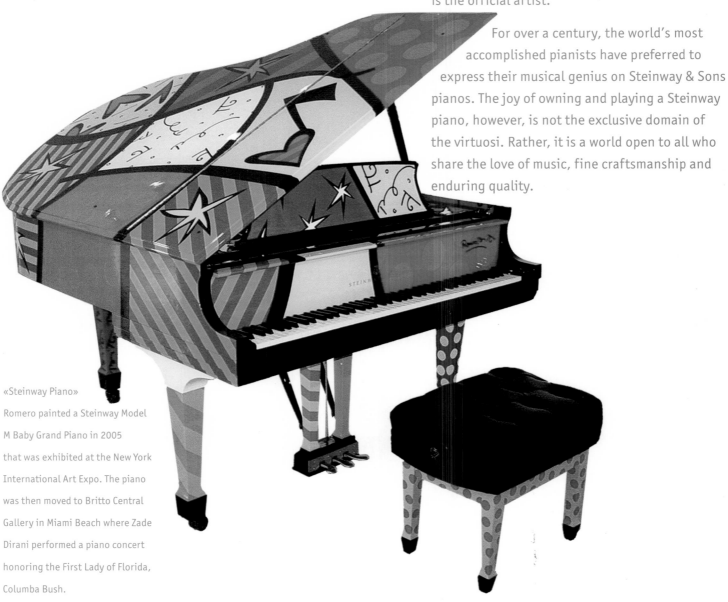

«Steinway Piano»

Romero painted a Steinway Model M Baby Grand Piano in 2005 that was exhibited at the New York International Art Expo. The piano was then moved to Britto Central Gallery in Miami Beach where Zade Dirani performed a piano concert honoring the First Lady of Florida, Columba Bush.

Romero painted a one-
of-a-kind Harley Davidson
Private Collection,
Rio de Janeiro, Brazil

Simplicity of a Genius

"The art of Romero Britto is simple: an explosion of basic colors, imprisoned in the limits of a talented black trace, distinguishes and personalizes it. Perhaps at first glance Britto's art will seem excessively simple. But, as constantly happens to refined and original works of art, every time that we try to imitate it, we find out how sophisticated and unique it is in its nuances and its meanings."

Alex Periscinoto
President of the 20 Biennale of São Paulo
Council of the Foundation Biennale of São Paulo

«São Paulo Stamps»
In 2004, Romero
was commissioned by
the State of São Paulo
to create four stamps
celebrating São Paulo's
450th Anniversary

450 ANOS DA CIDADE DE SÃO PAULO

1º Dia de Circulação

2010 FIFA WORLD CUP
SOUTH AFRICA

OFFICIAL ART POSTER
ROMERO BRITTO
SOUTH AFRICA 2010. 2009.

"Football is all about friendship and togetherness. This can start in the smallest community and spread throughout the country. It is humanity, people who are living their passion and who love to play. It's not really about winning or losing, but doing something you love. It is this spirit of celebration and sharing that brings people to the stadium. It really gets the emotions flowing." – Romero Britto, 2009

In early 2009, BRITTO was asked by the Federation Internationale de Football Association (FIFA), to be one of the contemporary artists to create an image inspired by FIFA's flagship competition. Revenue from poster prints of the art will benefit FIFA's 20 Centre's for 2010 campaign to promote public health, education and football in disadvantaged communities across Africa.

In June 2009, at the opening ceremonies for the 59th FIFA Congress in Nassau, Bahamas, BRITTO, joined FIFA Secretary General Jerome Valcke on stage in front of the FIFA congress to present his piece titled, South Africa 2010. "I was very excited to be asked to do that painting," said BRITTO, "Africa as a whole is a fascinating continent - it was the birthplace of civilization and will once again be the setting for a new beginning. Sport is a medium; it is humanity, a way to unite people. On the field, everyone is equal and can express themselves freely. The 2010 World Cup will be an opportunity for the world to get to know Africa as a whole, beginning with South Africa."

Much to BRITTO's surprise, FIFA Secretary General Jérôme Valcke then decided onstage that FIFA would buy the second piece BRITTO had created and make an additional donation of 100,000 USD to the 20 Centres for 2010 campaign. "We began this campaign by deciding to donate USD 500 for each goal scored during the qualifying competition for South Africa 2010. But I think we can do even better than that, which is why FIFA is going to donate USD 100,000," he said. BRITTO's piece titled South Africa 2010 is the first of the art collection on exhibit at the FIFA Headquarters in Zurich, Switzerland.

During the games, BRITTO traveled to Johannesburg, South Africa to paint with 32 children from disadvantaged communities around the world. The paint workshop was to promote Football for Hope, a program that uses the power of football for social development, led by Fifa. "Fifa is playing a genuine role in inspiring these children," declared BRITTO, "their presence here, together, is a great success because they come from all over the world, and will return home, happy and conscious of having an important role to play. They will speak with their families and friends about their experiences, and it will undoubtedly have an impact on their societies. I hope other organizations follow in FIFA's footsteps. When you enjoy success, you need to share it with others and there's no doubt, that FIFA is one of the most successful organizations around."

NORTH STAR

Romero Britto's "NORTH STAR" now greets visitors and locals alike as they enter Miami Beach via the McArthur Causeway at the corner of 5th and Alton. This 35 foot sculpture is commissioned by art collector and developer Jeffrey Berkowitz.

« North Star » 2010

Palm Trees 35 feet

Beach Ball 10 feet

SUPER BOWL XLI

February 3, 2007 900 million football fans around the world witnessed
history in the making, as Britto and Cirque Du Soleil joined forces to
create the first ever theatrical pre-game show performance kicking off
the SuperBowl XLI in Miami.

BRITTO
IN HYDE PARK

For the first time ever...
A visual artist has been invited to install a monumental
sculpture in historic Hyde Park.

Romero Britto, known around the world for his use of vivid colors and bold images, has designed a 45ft commemorative pyramid sculpture celebrating Tutankhamun's return to London after 35 years. Located at the world famous Speaker's Corner, the monumental sculpture was created using state-of-the-art composite materials by Innovida. The Britto pyramid is the largest art installation in the history of Hyde Park. It was produced in tribute to the Ancient Pyramids of Giza, the last of the remaining Seven Wonders of the World, and is scheduled to be permanently installed at the Children's Museum in Cairo, Egypt. Visitors to London from around the world also had an opportunity to see a 25ft pyramid at The O_2 through Spring 2008. A 4ft pyramid was also recently displayed at the British Museum. This pyramid installation celebrates the return of the King Tutankhamun exhibition to the United Kingdom.

Evian, the world's most
prestigious water bottling
company, commissioned
Romero Britto to design
several unique labels
for their brand.

Romero Britto with his son Brendan.

«MILLIE THE BUNNY» 2008
54" x 35" x 12"
Property of the White House National Archives
Romero Britto participated in the 2008
Easter Egg Roll with the first
sculpture for this event.

85

THE WHITE HOUSE

Princess Diana

THE PORTRAIT COLLECTION BY ROMERO BRITTO

In 2007, Romero Britto created a collection of portraits of the late Princess Diana showing the grace, strength and beauty of this great lady in each milestone of her life. The canvases were autographed by several of the Princess's friends and supporters including Anthony Hopkins, Columba & Jeb Bush, Celine Dion, Maria Shriver, Farah Diva, David Caruso, Liza Minelli, Frank Gehry and Hillary Clinton. In November all the artworks were unveiled in Paris where 100% of the proceeds for the sale of the works were donated to the Princess Diana Memorial Foundation and the International Campaign to Ban Landmines.

Romero Britto

in his studio

2007

«OLYMPIC SWIMMER» 2007
60" x 90", AC

P E A C E

THE UNITED NATIONS teams up with Romero Britto to commemorate the 2008 Beijing Summer Olympics with a limited stamp series themed "Sport for Peace." The second collaboration for Britto and the UN Postal Administration (UNPA), six new designs which showcase tennis, track, and gymnastics, celebrate the remarkable talent of the athletes in these games. The overall theme and slogan for the Beijing 2008 Olympic Games is "One World One Dream" which fully reflects the essence and the universal values of the Olympic spirit – Unity, Friendship, Progress, Harmony, Participation and Dream. "Britto created art pieces with a continuous message of hope," states the United Nations Postal Administration and a partnership on this project between the two became obvious and effortless. "Working on these five different artworks allowed me to spend a lot of time reflecting on the importance of goals and our ability to push ourselves to seemingly impossible limits." Romero Britto

BRITTO
AT THE LOUVRE

Romero Britto was invited to participate by the President of the Brazilian Delegation, Bia Duarte, in a show at the Salon Nationale Des Beaux-Arts 2008 in the Carrousel Du Louvre, Paris.

Commissioned in 2009 by world renowned developers of Resorts World Sentosa Romero Britto created a career collection of thirteen monumental sculpture highlighted by the crowning installation of five MEGA sculptures measuring over seven meters in height. Britto was asked to commission an additional original work to grace the hotel lobby. This triptych entitled "Sentosa Neverland" greets visitors upon their entry to Sentosa Resort.

Sentosa, which translates to peace and tranquility in Malay, is a popular island resort in Singapore, visited by over 8 million people a year.

« Sentosa Neverland » 2010

60" x 180", ADR

«Landscape» 1990

90˝ x 36˝, AC

Private Collection,

USA

96

«Untitled» 1991
60˝ x 48˝, AC
Private Collection,
USA

Romero ©1990

Romero Britto
© 1990

«Untitled» 1990

«Cheryl While the World Sleeps» 1993

80˝x 96˝, AC

Private Collection,

Belgium

«Untitled» 1993

24″ x 30″, AC

«Yellow Moon» 1991
80˝ x 60˝, AC
Collection of Alexander
Chistyakov, Moscow,
Russia

"Britto's work, «Rose's View»,
is a wonderful rendering of
my home in Hyannis Port. It is
colorful, lyrical and captures in a
unique way, the vivid memories
of the many wonderful times my
family and I have spent there.
I love it!"

Senator Edward M. Kennedy,
US Senator from Massachusetts

«Cutting Trees» 1992

72˝ x 72˝, AC

Private Collection,

USA

108

«It's Okay» 1992

48˝ x 60˝, AC

Private Collection,

Chicago, USA

«Rothschild Butterfly»

Collection of Baroness

Phillipine de Rothschild,

France

«Spotlight Mickey», 72˝ x 60˝
Painted to commemorate the 70th
Birthday of Disney's Mickey Mouse character,
this painting now resides in the Collection
of Mr. and Mrs. Edward Minskoff,
New York, USA

«Ruvo Girls» 1996

80″ x 96″, AC

Collection of Mr. and Mrs. Larry Ruvo,

Las Vegas, USA

«When I'm Away» 1995

60˝ x 96˝, AC

Private Collection,

Amsterdam, Netherlands

«Britto Wall» 1995

72″ x 72″, AC

Private Collection,

Singapore

114

«Cheryl Naked» 1995

48″ x 60″, AC

Collection of National

Museum of Art,

Rio de Janeiro, Brazil

115

«Cheek to Cheek»
Collection of Steffi Graf
and André Agassi,
Las Vegas, USA

«Camile» 1996

60″ x 90″, AC

Collection of Mr. and Mrs. Larry Ruvo,

Las Vegas, USA

117

«Pepsi» 1995

80˝ x 96˝, AC

Collection of Pepsi Company,

New York, USA

«Pepsi Taste» 1995

48″ x 60″, AC

Collection of Pepsi Company,

New York, USA

119

«New Generation» 1995

48˝x 60˝, AC

Collection of Pepsi Company,

New York, USA

«Ms. Miranda» 1995

60˝x 48˝, AC

Private Collection,

USA

«Samba» 1995

72˝ x 72˝, AC

Private Collection,

USA

«On Top of the World» 1995

72″ x 72″, AC

Private Collection,

São Paulo, Brazil

«Don't Tread on Me» 1995

48˝ x 60˝, AC

Private Collection,

Austria

«The Blue Monkey» 1995

48˝ x 60˝, AC

Collection of Kalamazoo Institute of Arts,

Michigan, USA

«Flowers for You» 1995

72˝ x 72˝, AC

Private Collection,

USA

126

«Fine Romance» 1995

80˝ x 90˝, AC

Private Collection,

USA

«Holland» 1997

48˝ x 36˝, AC

Private Collection,

Germany

«Brendan's Cat» 1996

36˝ x 48˝, AC

Private Collection,

USA

«Bowling Angel» 1995

72˝ x 72˝, AC

Private Collection,

São Paulo, Brazil

130

«Brendan and I» 1995

60″ x 48″, AC

Private Collection,

USA

«Octopus» 1995

80″ x 96″, AC

Collection of Mr. and Mrs. Levine,

USA

132

«Colors of Brazil» 1995

80˝ x 96˝, AC

Collection of Fernando Collor de Mello,

Former President of Brazil

«The Apple» 1996

32˝ x 32˝, AC

Private Collection,

Tokyo, Japan

«Singing Bird» 1996

72˝ x 72˝, AC

Collection of Mr. and Mrs. Stulman,

Las Vegas, USA

«Love Blossoms» 1998
80˝ x 96˝, AC
Private Collection,
Miami, USA

«The Red Hair» 2000

60˝ x 48˝, AC

Private Collection,

USA

138

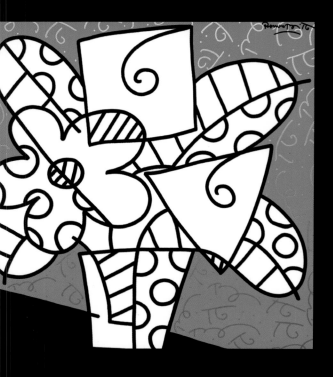

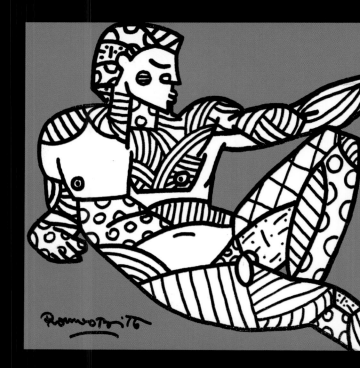

«Aqua Flowers» 2002

48˝ x 48˝, ADR

Private Collection,

USA

«David» 20

8˝ x 10˝, A

Private Collecti

«About Picasso» 2003

«Venus» 2003

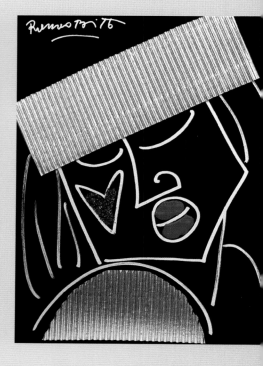

«Night Love» 2003

22″ x 20″, ADR

The Artist's Collection,

USA

«Night Flower» 2003

20″ x 22″, ADR

The Artist's Collection,

USA

«Feeling Good» 2003

22″ x 20″, ADR

The Artist's Collection,

USA

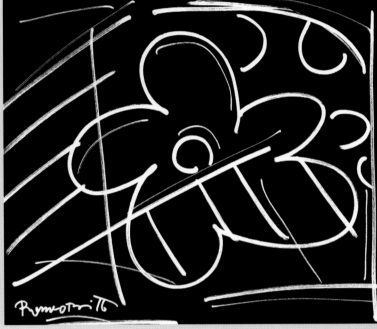

«Black Cat» 2003

20˝ x 22˝, ADR

The Artist's Collection,

USA

«Night Spring» 2003

20˝ x 22˝, ADR

The Artist's Collection,

USA

«Two in Love» 2004

48″ x 60″, ADR

Collection of Rainer Martin,

Switzerland

144

«Free Trial Offer» 2007

48" x 60", ADR

145

«Love Life»
This original painting was donated
to the Braman Family Breast Cancer Institute
to help in raising funds for breast cancer
research and awareness.

«The Solomons», 2000

80˝ x 96˝, AC

Collection of Mr. and Mrs. Solomon,

Boca Raton,

Florida, USA

147

Painted in homage

to soccer legend, Pelé

Painted in homage
to soccer legend, Pelé

Painted in homage
to soccer legend,
Pelé

«Modern Day - Tristan & Isolde» 2010
80" x 96", ADR

«Miami Sensation» 2005

24˝ x 36˝, CDC

Collection of Karin and

Dieter Randegger,

Switzerland

«Royality» 2005

30˝ x 24˝, ADR

Private Collection,

USA

«Cheryl's Cat» 2007

47" x 41", AOW

«Deeply in Love»

92˝ x 153˝, AC

Collection of Family Rohr,

Switzerland

«Untitled» 2008
72" x 72", ADR

«Bacardi Commission» 2004

48˝ x 60˝, AC

Collection of Facundo Bacardi,

Miami, USA

«Children of the World», 2005
AC
Romero painted this original
image for Best Buddies International. The painting will
be reproduced for new release
serigraphs. Profits from
the sale of the serigraphs will
benefit Best Buddies.

«I Love This Land» 2005

36″ x 48″, ADR

Collection of Mr. & Mrs. Sheldon

Adelson, USA

Romero created this original
piece to raise funds for the
Israel Defense Forces.

162

«Columba Bush» 2005

40″ x 30″, ADR

Romero Britto painted a

portrait of beloved friend

and Florida's First Lady

Columba Bush.

«Claudia & Guy» 2005

30″ x 36″, ADR

Collection of Guy La Liberte,

Montreal, Canada

165

«Love & Star» 2005

48˝ x 48˝, AC

Private Collection,

USA

166

«Waiting» 2005
60˝ x 36˝
Collection of
Family Brenner,
Switzerland

167

«New Underwear» 2005

40″ x 30″, ADR

The Artist's Collection,

USA

«Let me Think» 2005

30˝ x 40˝, ADR

Opera Gallery Collection,

Singapore

«South Beach Swimmer» 2005

40˝ x 30˝, ADR

Private Collection,

USA

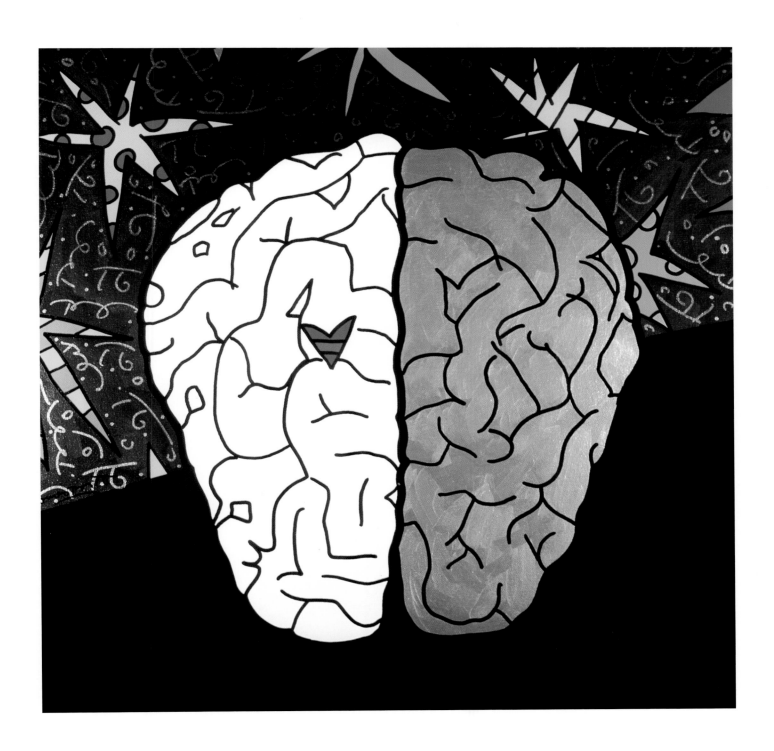

«Beautiful Mind» 2005

40˝ x 40˝, ADR

Private Collection,

USA

«Mona Cat» 2004
40″ x 32″, AB
Private Collection,
USA

«Tokyo» 2006

36" x 36", ADR

«Outdoors» 2005

48˝ x 60˝, AC

Private Collection,

USA

174

«Summer of Love» 2007

72" x 72", ADR

«Love is in the Air» 2006

75˝ x 60˝, ADR

Collection Family Rohr,

Switzerland

«On Top of the World» 2006

48˝ x 60˝, ADR

Collection of Scott and Michelle Tesser,

New Jersey, USA

«Keuka Lake» 2006

108˝ x 54˝, ADR

Private Collection,

Germany

178

«Kid» 2006

48˝ x 48˝, AC

Private Collection,

USA

«Pink Girl» 2006

48˝ x 48˝, AC

Private Collection,

USA

«Mother» 2006
40″ x 30″, ADR
Private Collection,
USA

«So Happy» 2006

72˝ x 72˝, AC

Private Collection,

USA

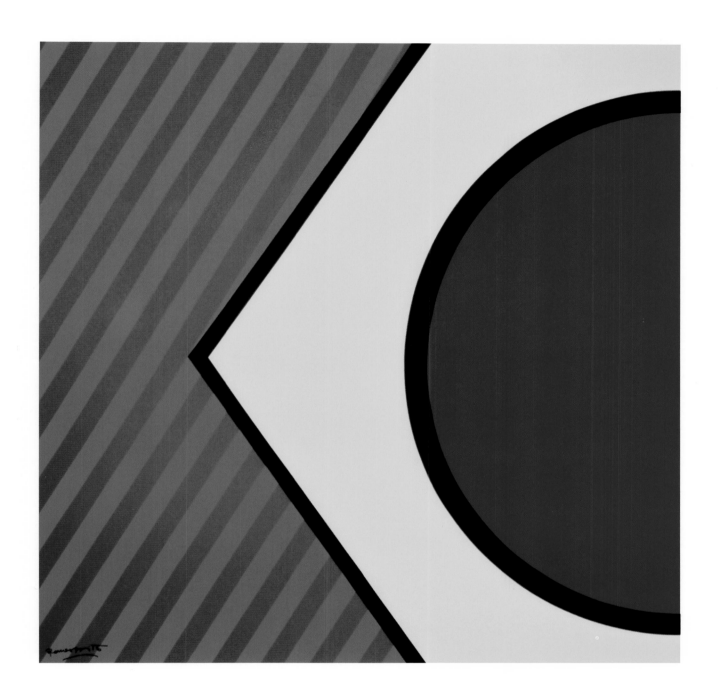

«Brazilian Flag» 2005

48″ x 48″, AC

Collection of the artist,

USA

«Plus» 2006

48˝ x 48˝, AC

Collection of the artist,

USA

«Victor and Muriel» 2005

30″ x 40″, ADR

Collection of Mr. and Mrs. Jorg Horn,

Germany

185

«CMC» 2005

44 x 43 cm, Sculpture,

Enamel on aluminum

Edition of 100

«For You» 2005

21 x 21 cm, Sculpture,

Enamel on aluminum

Edition of 100

«Mini Apple» 2005

14 x 23 cm, Sculpture,

Enamel on aluminum

Edition of 100

«Mini Fish» 2005

14 x 23 cm, Sculpture,

Enamel on aluminum

Edition of 100

«Cat» 2006

Wood sculpture

Collection of Marianne Akeret,

Switzerland

Edition of 100

«Dog» 2006

Wood sculpture

Collection of Marianne Akeret,

Switzerland

Edition of 100

«Teddy Bear» 2006

Wood sculpture

Edition of 100

«Madonna» 2008

36" x 48", ADR

«Madonna» 2008
36" x 48", ADR

«Cheryl at Hemingway Garden» 2006

48˝ x 60˝, ADR

Collection of the artist,

USA

192

«Brendan» 2002

48˝ x 60˝, ADR

Collection of the artist,

USA

«World Economy» 2008

36" x 48", ADR

194

ROMERO BRITTO creates a completely new expression that reflects his optimistic faith in the world around him. Eileen Guggenheim wrote it best when stating "Chagall's floating lovers seem to foreshadow so many of Britto's buoyant exultant couples." Alluding to influences of early and modern masters, Britto's pulsating colors, pop themes and commanding compositions have led him to become the premier contemporary Artist of his generation.

ROMERO BRITTO lived an extremely modest lifestyle while growing up amongst eight brothers and sisters in Recife Brazil. However, his innate creativity allowed Britto to fill his life with vibrant color and images of a beautiful world. His canvas was any scrap of newspaper or cardboard he could find. Britto has an inordinate passion to excel and prospered academically. Still, Britto's artistic nature eventually led him to seek experiences outside the classroom.

ROMERO BRITTO traveled to Europe in 1983 to examine firsthand the Art of the masters. After exhibiting in a few galleries and private shows, Britto was encouraged to travel to the United States where Pop Art was flourishing. Britto moved to Miami and set up a studio open to the public. With an unshakable resolve and belief in his art, Britto spent the next few years exhibiting and attracting the attention of many. Then, in 1989, Absolut Vodka® selected Britto to design an artwork with their famous logo. Britto's participation added his name to a list of Artists, such as Warhol and Haring, also commissioned for the famed vodka campaign. Britto's studio in Miami Beach was quickly becoming known as the place for people of all ages and walks of life to meet and acquire a unique style of art.

ROMERO BRITTO today is represented in galleries and museums across five continents. Opening in Paris at the Salle le Nôtre, Louvre Museum in December 2008, Britto unveiled "Journey" to hundreds of guests. Other unique artistic endeavors have flourished. "...Matisse channeling Picasso," wrote the New York Times® when Britto created a living canvas performed by the Cirque du Soleil in celebration of Super Bowl XLI.

ROMERO BRITTO artwork on canvas have found the spotlight in numerous corporate commissions and noted art collections. Britto's repertoire includes likenesses of the late Ernest Beyeler, founder of Art Basel as well as the late Robert Rauschenberg. Over 20 cities have Britto sculpture as permanent installations. And, Britto is the first artist to display monumental sculpture in Hyde Park, London. His diverse resume also includes several series of postage stamp designs for the United Nations Postal Administration and a postage stamp in Brazil that celebrates the 450th Anniversary of the city of Sao Paulo. In 2010, Romero Britto will launch his first children's book, "My Alphabet Playbook" that will lead children through a colorful collection of artistic learning.

ROMERO BRITTO is an artistic activist for charitable organizations worldwide and most of all an artist who believes "art is too important not to share." Britto donates to over 250 charitable organizations a year. Not a silent activist, Britto was a selected speaker for the arts at the World Economic Forum in Davos, Switzerland in 2006, '07, '09 and '10. Further, this year Romero Britto is proudly an Inaugural Founding Benefactor of the Harvard International Negotiation Program. Britto is committed to developing and supporting the powerful role art will continue to play in world issues.

2010 Gallery Petrus, San Juan, Puerto Rico, Opera Gallery, Hong Kong, S.A.R, Gallerie Mensing, Berlin, Germany, The Gallery, Mexico City Of Mexico, D'griss Fine Art, Panama, Benemerita Universidad, Autonoma De Puebla, Puebla, Mexico. **2009** Emirate's Palace Hotel, Abu Dubai, United Arab Emirates, Opera Gallery, Dubai, United Arab Emirates, Coral Springs Museum Of Art, Miami, Florida, Opera Gallery, New York, Galleria On 3rd, New York, Galerie Mensing, Hamburg, Germany, Galerie Mensing, Dusseldorf, Germany, Galerie Mensing, Hamm-Rhynem Germany, Tratzberg Castle, Jenbach, Austria, VW Automobile Forum, Berlin, Germany, Audi Exhibit, Santiago, Chile, Opera Gallery, Singapore, Opera Gallery, Seoul, South Korea, Egan Maritime Institute, Nantucket, Massachusetts, Monteux Jazz Festival 2009, Switzerland, Opera, London, England, Naples Botanical Gardens, Naples, Florida. **2008** Opera Gallery, London, England, Kimhyunjoo Gallery, South Korea, Galerie Mensing, Germany, Opera Gallery, Singapore, DDR Sculpture Tour, United States, Louvre Museum, Salle de Norte, Paris, France, Museum Of Guangzhou Art Academy, Guangzhou, China, RCM Gallery, Nanjing, China, Sichuan Fine Arts Museum, Chengdu, Sichuan, China, Today Art Museum, Beijing, China. **2007** New York Art Expo, New York, Galerie Mensing, Frankfurt, Germany, Galerie Mensing, Berlin, Germany, Galerie Mensing, Dusseldorf, Germany, S2 Art Group, Las Vegas, Nevada, Opera Gallery, Hong Kong, S.A.R, Atlas Gallery, Chicago, Illinois, Las Vegas International Art Expo, Las Vegas, Nevada, Museum Of Contemporary Art MOCA, Shanghai, China. **2006** Florida House, Washington, Dc, Serendipity Fine Art, Palm Beach, Florida, New York International Art Exp, New York, Sundook Fine Art, Boca Raton, Florida, Galerie Mensing, Frankfurt, Germany, Galerie Mensing, Dusseldorf, Germany, Galerie Mensing, Munich, Germany, Park West Galleries, Southfield, Michigan, Art Basel, Basel, Switzerland, Montreux Jazz Festival, Montreux, Switzerland, Ravelo Festival, Florence, Italy, Galerie Ficher Rohr, Basel, Switzerland. **2005** Galerie Ficher Rohrbasel, Switzerland, Galerie Mensing, Munich, Germany, Galerie Mensing, Berlin, Germany, Galerie Mensing, Hamm, Germany, Galerie Mensing, Dusseldorf, Germany, Galerie Mensing, Hamburg, Germany, International Biennale Of Contemporary Art, Florence, Italy, New York Art Expo, New York, Opera Gallery, Bal Harbour, Florida, Opera Gallery, New York, Opera Gallery, Singapore, Opera Gallery, Paris, France. **2004** Artevista, Amsterdam, Holland, Atlas Gallery, Chicago, Illinois, Enrico Coveri Showroom, Florence, Italy, Galerie Mensing, Germany, La Maison De L'Amérique Latine, Monte Carlo, Monaco, New York Art Expo, New York, Sala Garzanti, Milan, Italy. **2003** Galerie Mensing, Audi Event Germany Arte Vista, Nan Miller Gallery, Rochester, New York, New York Art Expo, New York, Opera Gallery, New York, The Pop Art Gallery, Badhoevedorp, Amsterdam. **2002** Coral Springs Museum Of Art, Coral Springs, Florida, Ct Atlas Gallery, Chicago, Illinois, Galerie Mensing, Berlin, Germany, Galerie Mensing, Hamburg, Germany, Galerie Mensing, Hamm, Germany, Nan Miller Gallery, Rochester, New York, New York Art Expo, New York, Opera Gallery, Singapore, Penn Yann Gallery, Penn Yann, New York. **2001** Artmosphere Gallery, South Hampton, New York, Britto Central Sao Paulo, São Paulo, Brazil, Finelot Galleries St., James, London, England, Galerie Mensing, Germany, Galerie Mensing, Hamburg, Germany, Galerie Mensing, Hamm, Germany, Gallery One, Los Angeles, California, Lavon Art Gallery, Morganville, New Jersey, Nan Miller Gallery, Rochester, New York, New York Art Expo, New York. **2000** Art Mode, Calgary, Canada, Finelot London, England, Gallery Richter, Berlin, Germany, Lavon Gallery, Morganville, New Jersey, Nan Miller Gallery, Rochester, New York, New York Art Expo, New York, Peter Gwyther, London, England, Pop International, New York, New York, Sundook Art Gallery, Boca Raton, Florida, Syd Entel Gallery, Tampa, Florida. **1999** Art 21, Las Vegas, Nevada, Art Mode, Calgary, Canada, Art Trend Graz, Vienna, Salzburg, Austria, Foxx Gallery, Zurich, Switzerland, Liss Gallery, Toronto, Canada, Nan Miller Gallery, Rochester, New York, New York Art Expo, New York, October Gallery, London, England, Pop International, New York, Qualita Fine Art, Las Vegas, Nevada, Sundook Gallery, Boca Raton, Florida. **1998** Art Space, Hong Kong, China, Art Expo, New York, Barucci Gallery, Clayton, Missouri, Disney Gallery, New York, Galerie Blu, Birmingham, Michigan, Galleria Prova, Tokyo, Japan, Herman Krause, Munich, Germany, Karen Jenkins Johnson, San Francisco, California, Kenneth Behm Gallery, Bellvue, Washington, Lavon Art Gallery, East Brunswick, New Jersey, Museo De Arte E Historia, San Juan, Puerto Rico, Nan Miller Gallery, Rochester, New York, Nature Gallery, Tumon, Guam, Newbury Fine Art, Boston, Massachusetts, Pop International, New York, Sky Art, Knokke, Belgium. **1997** American Art Company, Tacoma, Washington, Art Un, Chigasaki: Kanagawa Prefecture, Japan, Best Buddies Art Company, Miami Beach, Florida, Galerie Blu, Birmingham, Michigan, Galleria Prova, Tokyo, Japan, Herman,

Krause, Cologne, Germany, Just Looking Gallery, San Obispo, California, New York Art Expo, New York, Newbury Fine Art, Boston, Massachusetts, Nuance Galleries, Tampa, Florida, Odakyu Museum, Tokyo, Japan, Star Gallery, Bern, Switzerland, Sundook Art Galleries, Boca Raton, Florida, Suppan Fine Art, Vienna, Austria, Vancouver International Arts Exhibition, Vancouver, British Columbia, Art America, Vancouver, British Columbia, Z Gallery, Fukuoka, Japan. **1996** Art Americas, Nan Miller Gallery: Miami, Florida, Art Miami, Nan Miller Gallery: Miami, Florida, Art Expo New York, New York, Britto Central, Miami Beach, Florida, Fine Arts Museum Of Long Island, Hempstead, New York, Florida Museum Of Hispanic & Latin American Art, Miami, Florida, Galleria Prova, Aoyama Gallery: Minato-Ku Tokyo, Japan, Galleria Prova, Bunko-Ku Tokyo, Japan, Galleria Prova, Hotel Bleston Court, Karuizawamachi: Nagona, Japan, Galleria Prova, Tokyo, Japan, Lineart, Ghent, Belgium, Masterpiece Galleries, Boca Raton, Florida, Museo Del Nino, Caracas, Venezuela, Stricoff Fine Art Gallery, New York, Studio of Long Grove, Long Grove, Illinois, Westwood Gallery, New York, Women's International, Zionist Organization Art Exhibit: Aventura, Florida. **1995** Art Americas, Nan Miller Gallery: Miami, Florida, Art Miami, Nan Miller Gallery: Miami, Florida, Britto Central, Miami, Florida, Castelli Graphics, Bailey House: New York, New York, Fay Gold Gallery, Atlanta, Georgia, Galleria Renato Goureia de Megalhaes Lineart, Ghent, Belgium, Nan Miller Gallery, Rochester, New York, New Trends Hong Kong, Nan Miller Gallery: Hong Kong, Suppan Fine Arts, Vienna, Austria. **1994** Art Asia, Hong Kong, Art Cologne, Cologne, Germany, Art Fair Seattle, Nan Miller Gallery: Seattle, Washington, Art Miami, Miller Gallery: Miami, Florida, Arte Fiera, Bologna, Italy, Artisma Torino, Turin, Italy, Britto Central, Miami Beach, Florida, Buschlen-Mowett, Vancouver, British Columbia, Ekerum, Konst Hall: Oland, Sweden, Emery Fine Arts, Portage, Michigan, FIAC, Grana Palais: Paris, France, FIAC, Trésors, Singapore, Jan Price Art Associates, Syracuse, New York, Kass Meridian Gallery, Chicago, Illinois, Lineart, Ghent, Belgium, Nan Miller Gallery, Rochester, New York, Stricoff Fine Art Gallery, New York, Wentworth Galleries, Short Hills, New Jersey, Wentworth Galleries, Roosevelt, Long Island, Wentworth Galleries, Boca Raton, Florida. **1993** Art Asia, Kass/Meridian Gallery: Hong Kong, Art Bogota, Kass/Meridian Gallery: Bogotá, Colombia, Art Chicago, Kass/Meridian Gallery: Chicago, Illinois, Art Fair Seattle, Nan Miller Gallery: Seattle, Washington, Art Miami, Nan Miller Gallery: Miami, Florida, Arte Fiera, Kass Meridian Gallery: Bologne, Italy, Caracas Expo, Kass/Meridian: Caracas, Venezuela, FIAC, The Grande Palais/Meridian Gallery: Paris, France, Harrington Fine Art Gallery, Vancouver, Canada, Kass/Meridian Gallery, Chicago, Illinois, Lineart, Ghent, Belgium, MBCC Maastricht Expo, Maastricht, Holland, Stricoff Fine Art Gallery, New York. **1992** Absolut Exhibition, Tokyo, Japan, Absolut Vodka Exhibition, Casa Ricardo: São Paulo, Brazil, Art Miami, Miami, Florida, American Artists Exhibition, French Embassy: New York, New York, Candido Mendes Cultural Center, Rio De Janeiro, Brazil, Fine Arts Museum Of Long Island, Hempstead, New York, Montana University, Bozeman, Montana, Philadelphia Art Show, Philadelphia, Pennsylvania, Stricoff Fine Art Gallery, New York, Sunday By The Bay Aids Benefit Exhibition, Long Island, New York, The Nan Miller Gallery, Rochester, New York, The Rocky Aoki Collection, Tokyo, Japan. **1991** Art Miami, Miami, Florida, Candide Gallery, Atlanta, Georgia, Coral Gables Fine Arts Gallery, Miami, Florida, Coral Snake Gallery, Miami Beach, Florida, Degraaf Gallery, Chicago, Illinois, Degraaf Gallery, Costa Mesa, California, Earth Train Exhibition, United Nations Plaza: New York, New York, Morel Company, Exhibition Of Britto's Grand Marnier Collection: New York, Philadelphia Art Show, Philadelphia, Pennsylvania, Sunday-By-The-Bay Aids Benefit Exhibition, Long Island, New York. **1990-1986** Artists For Amnesty, Amnesty International (Leo Catelli's Exhibit Of Featured Artists): New York, Café Des Arts Gallery, South Miami Beach, Florida, Hotel Softie Bastille Day Exhibit, Miami, Florida, Hotel Softie Brazilian Independence Day Exhibit, Miami, Florida, Hyatt Regency Hotel Art Showcase, Miami, Florida, Offens Atelier, Erlangen, Germany, Public Works Department, Stangnas, Sweden, Queen Charlotte Hall, London, England, The Bayside Gallery, Miami, Florida, The Mayfair Gallery "Absolut Britto Exhibit", Miami, Florida, The Mayfair Gallery, Miami, Florida, The Mayfair Gallery, Miami, Florida, Whiting Hall, Sunrise, Florida, Wirtz Gallery, Miami, Florida. **1989** Body Positive Benefit Exhibition, Wolfsonian Foundation: Miami Beach, Florida. **1988** National Conference of Professors Exhibition, University of Miami: Miami, Florida. 1986 Kultuhucet Exhibit, Stockholm, Sweden. **1985** "Revivendo Bandeira" Unicap Museum of Brazil, Recife, Brazil, Annual International Club Exhibition, Recife, Brazil, Contemporary Brazilian Artists, Governor's Residence: Pernambuco, Brazil. **1979** Organization of American States Exhibition, Brasilia, Brazil.

Romero Britto and
Countess Beatriz
de Bourbon

Famous Israeli artist,
Jacob Agam and
Duke Zimmerman,
looking at Romero's
artwork

Bianca Jagger
and Romero Britto at
the Kennedy Center in
Washington, DC

Anthony and
Alina Shriver with
Romero Britto

Elton John and
Romero Britto in
Las Vegas while Elton
John autographed
Romero's pieces
for the André Agassi
Foundation

Japanese artist
Hiro Yamagata and
Romero Britto

Issey Miyake
attending the first
Britto opening
in Tokyo

Romero Britto
and actress
Kathleen Turner in
the Hamptons,
New York

Marlo Thomas hosts
exhibition for Britto
at Pop International
in New York City

Jeffrey Newhouse
visiting Britto
at an opening in
New York City

Celebrated
brazilian architect,
Oscar Niemeyer
receives Romero for
an afternoon
Brazilian coffee

200

Marta Suplicy,
former Mayor of São Paulo
at Britto Central
in São Paulo, Brazil

Ivana Trump hosts
party for Britto
at Pop International
in New York

Evander Holyfield at the
after-party of Romero's
exhibition in the Fay Gold
Gallery, Atlanta

Romero with artist
Chuck Close

Romero and
soccer legend
Pelé

Emeril Lagasse,
Alden Lagasse and
Romero Britto

Mickey Mouse's first
trip to South America.
Mickey came for
the opening of Romero
Britto's exhibition at the
Museum of Modern Art
in Rio de Janeiro.

   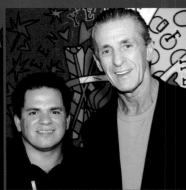

Romero Britto,
Frank Gehry and Chef
Nobu Matsuhisa

Romero Britto and
Arnold Schwarzenegger

Larry Ruvo, Maria Shriver,
Arnold Schwarzenegger
and Romero Britto take
a look at a model of the
Larry Ruvo Foundation's
new facility designed
by architect, Frank Gehry

Romero Britto and
legendary basketball
coach, Pat Riley

André Agassi
and Romero Britto in
Romero's studio

Romero Britto
with Norman and
Irma Braman

Ronaldo
and his Britto

204

Mikhail Gorbachev
reflecting on
a Britto piece

Guggenheim at
Rockefeller Center.
Richard Ziegelasch,
Romero Britto, Anthony
Kennedy-Shriver &
Eileen Guggenheim
lunching at Rockefeller
Center in New York

The great American
artist Robert Rauschenberg
with Romero. Both painters
were in Dubai to attend
a benefit for the international organization,
Doctors without Borders.

Romero Britto
and Gai Mattiolo,
the new Valentino
of Rome

Romero Britto
was appointed
Florida Ambassador
of the Arts, 2005

Romero Britto with
former U.S. President
Bill Clinton

Banker Joseph Safra
and a Britto in
São Paulo, Brazil

Peggy Iacocca
and Romero

Senator Edward Kennedy
commissioned a piece
for the family house in
Hyannis Port where the
Kennedys have spent their
summers for decades

Romero, Carlos Slim
and Anthony Shriver
in Mexico.

Romero with Mr. and
Mrs. Facundo Bacardi

Morris Lapidus,
contemporary architect
and Romero Britto

Hispanic Heritage Month.
Governor of Florida
Jeb Bush, First Lady of
Florida Columba Bush
and Romero Britto at the
Hispanic Heritage Month
celebration where
they honored Romero
as the 2004/2005
Ambassador of the Arts

Romero laughing
with Baroness
Phillipine de Rothschild
after presenting
her with the painting
«Rothschild Butterfly»

Jeff Koons and
Romero Britto with
Fabiola Beracasa
in Palm Beach

First Lady, Hillary Clinton and
Romero after unveiling a
mural at St. Jude Children's
Research Hospital in
Memphis, Tennessee

Romero and gallery
staff at his exibition
at Gallery Prova in
Tokyo, Japan

Juli, Justin and
Edward Minskoff in
Romero's Studio in
Miami Beach

Romero and Carlos
Alberto Parreira,
Brazilian Soccer Coach
in São Paulo, Brazil

Romero and
Princess Gloria von
Thurn und Taxis

Romero and
Chancellor of Germany
Angela Merkel
in Berlin

Romero Britto
at the White House,
Spring 2006

Romero, President Barack
Obama and Brendan Britoo
Miami, Florida, USA

Romero Britto
Around the world

Romero speaking at
Georgetown University
Washington, DC, USA

Romero and
Michael Jackson
in Germany

Romero and King
Juan Carlos and
Queen Sofia of Spain
in Miami, Florida, USA

Jeb & Columba Bush,
President George H.W. Bush
& Barbara Bush, Romero
and Dorothy Bush Koch

Prince Charles, Prince of Wales
and Romero in London UK

Gisele Bundchen
and Romero in
Miami, Florida, USA

Romero George W. Bush
Laura Bush and Romero
in the White House
Washington, DC, USA

"'Life's happiness depends on the nature of your thoughts' said the Roman Emperor Marc Aurel. So what do Britto and Marc Aurel have in common? The last stoic of antiquity, Aurel, was drawn into numerous battles in defense of his empire but still maintained that each day be viewed as a gift and preached that the mighty should retain humility when facing their people. The contemporary artist also inspires the mind with his heartfelt affirmation of life which is reflected in his paintings that are passionately full of life and daringly colorful."

Georges Vanoncini

"«Love at first sight» would describe our reaction when we first encountered Romero Britto's paintings. We find his naturally winning, lovable charm irresistible, which reflected in his paintings and sculptures, brightens up our daily life with their cheerful radiance..."

Herbert and Susy Thaler

"We were immediately taken with the luminous colors and clear forms in Britto's work with its play of colors as well as the use of the apple motif in our painting «Waiting», which reminds us of the legend of Wilhelm Tell..."

Monika and Walter Brenner

"What appealed to us about Romero Britto's work is the joy that it expresses, the positive aura that flows from it, the choice of the charming themes and the pure saturated colors. It's not only his work that is authentic and honest, but also the artist himself with his genuine sincerity, modesty and an overwhelming charisma that has remained unchanged despite his success and fame..."

Hans and Marianne Akeret

"Romero is a messenger in the garden of humanity; what words fail to express about the joys and sufferings of life are reflected in his paintings and sculptures. His illustrations are impressive; here he considerably reduces the variations of color emphasizing mimicry and mood which in turn mesmerizes the viewer..."

Horst and Heidi Nickel

"Encountering Britto and his artwork is like discovering a semi-cut diamond on a gravel path. On the one hand we are confronted with perfection, brilliance, shining colors, transparency, exclusiveness and a unique quality, and on the other the characteristic of being, easy going, unconventional, innocently naïve and above all the characteristic of what appears on the surface as being unpretentious carries within its depths something pure and priceless..."

Peter Kern

"I've loved Romero's work for many years. As an amateur painter myself, I admire his dramatic use of color and his bold images. He is a talented artist and a treasured friend of the Kennedy Family."

Senator Edward M. Kennedy of Massachusetts

"The new sensibility, addressing itself to the contemporary clutter of sensory stimuli, is an odd reformation that reinterprets the need for content in terms that are visual instead of intellectual, sensuous rather than severe. Satiated with ideas, Romero Britto no longer wants a thinking art that needs to be read; he wants something pleasurable to look at again. If linguistic structure was a logical model for many artists in the previous decade, Britto is finding his models in the inchoate workings of the memory and psyche; in irrational splices and displacements, subliminal associations, discontinuous fragments whose connective logic has long since dissolved, and forms whose structural integrity is

a matter of faith. In his art, Britto is trying to integrate the abstract and the representational, the artificial and the natural, the replica and the original, wanting everything at once – and he is creating a truly synthetic art, in every sense of the word. On behalf of the Board of Trustees of the Boca Raton Museum of Art, I wish to express our sincere appreciation to Romero Britto for his unstinting enthusiasm and cooperation during the planning of this project. The Museum staff is grateful to him not only for his meticulous concern for the just presentation of his work, but for his ontological presence."

George S. Bolge,
Executive Director, Boca Raton Museum of Art

"Galleria Prova believes that Romero's work will be loved in Japan and will make a lasting impression as we speed into 21st Century."

Hiroki Suzuki, Galleria Prova, President

"Romero Britto's arrival in Florida, almost ten years ago, represents one of the most significant artistic contributions to a nearly culturally desolate milieu."

Raul M. Oyuela,
Director of the Florida Museum of Hispanic and Latin American Art

"Romero thank you very much for being a wonderful friend of MOCA! Your contribution and commitment to the museum has helped us grow tremendously and I'm thrilled that you are such a special part of MOCA. Many thanks! Congratulations on your stellar career!"

Bonnie Clearwater,
Director of the Museum of Contemporary Art, Miami, Florida

"Colors and shapes burst open and melt to form a bright and lively painting. Viewers can participate in the work just as the children in the hospital did. This is the style of Romero Britto's work."

Tetsuro Muobushi,
Writer, Critic and Editor of Prints 21

"Romero is the greatest living artist."

Facundo Bacardi,
Chairman of the Board, Bacardi & Company, the world's largest, privately-owned spirits company

"Romero Britto's art is colorful and innovative and most certainly distinctive. The entire family enjoys it a great deal."

Gloria Estefan

"Instead of donating checks, giving away his art is a more personal, more satisfying means of contributing to the community."

Rick Jervis, Miami Herald

"Highly collectible, Britto's work is the hottest ticket in town and on the collecting circuit."

Carol Carney, Ingrove Magazine

"When I think of Romero Britto and his inspiring work, it brings great joy, opportunity and spirit to me in a way that is unparalleled by any other. I hope a day will never pass that I don't have a chance to look at a Britto and smile."

Anthony Kennedy Shriver

"The colors that come from his inner soul and the perfection and details of his work are the reflection of his great talent. Born from humble beginnings, he has followed his destiny."

Fernando Collor de Mello, Former President of Brazil

Collectors' and Curators' Comments

"Romero your art is so colorful and Happy! You are universal!"

Carlos Slim

"Romero Britto navigates in an ocean of colors and arrives on an island of harmony."

Paulo Coelho

"To Romero Britto, the artist, our sincere appreciation for the contributions he has made to the United Nations stamps."

Kofi A. Annan

"The studio, the work ... it was a revelation to me!"

Morris Lapidus

"Romero is making a very positive impression upon the art world, as well as bringing joy to those fortunate enough to observe or own his works."

Senator Bob Graham

"An art of joy and pleasure – an art that appeals to so many people worldwide – this, indeed, is Romero Britto's great gift."

Eileen Guggenheim, PhD.

"You are truly a gifted man and continue to make me feel as though my artistic capabilities go no further than stick figures!"

John Pritzker

"Romero, you are magic."

Beatrice de Bourbon

"Romero Britto brings lively color and strong images to every idea he creates."

Rocky Aoki

"Your creativity on canvas is surpassed only by your kind nature and your vigorous support of worthwhile causes and charities."

Seymour Stein

"Romero, you deserve all your success."

Norman Braman

"Romero is a remarkable creator. I'm forever impressed by and love Romero's world."

Michiko Hatton

"We think you are a wonderful artist."

Elizabeth and Alfredo Beracasa

"It's amazing how I still get extremely excited over every work of art you create."

Tom Abraham

"Romero, you (your art) are in the business of transforming people to smile ... "

Klaus Schwab

"First, brilliant. That's the best word I know to characterize you. I am inspired by your way of understanding the world, and am excited to see where your creative energies take us." Romero Britto's work is expansive!"

Dr. Daniel Shapiro, Harvard University

"The work of Romero Britto is an expression of happiness and the best that humanity has to offer."

Columba Bush

"Romero, you smile with your eyes".

Colby (photographer - Miami New Times)

"Romero's art is a personification of himself, his heart, his soul, his

Romero Britto

"Happiness for me is the ability to appreciate the simple and